This book is dedicated to my family who has always supported me throughout my life's journey. Thank you for always believing in my potential.

Table of Contents

<u>Intro to Python</u>　　　　　　　　　　　Pg 11
　What is Python?

<u>Starting to Code</u>　　　　　　　　　　Pgs 13-17
　Where do I start coding?
　How do I run my code?
　Basic Python Things to be Familiar With
　Writing Comments

<u>Data Types</u>　　　　　　　　　　　　　Pgs 19-23
　String data type
　Integer data type
　Float data type
　Boolean data type
　Print statements

<u>More About Variables</u>　　　　　　　　Pgs 25-29
　Changing Variable Types
　Casting
　Obtaining a Variable's Type

Table of Contents

Naming Variables
Variable Shortcut
Print Shortcut

<u>Operators</u>   Pgs 31-34
  What is an Operator?
  Arithmetic Operators
  Modulus
  Exponents
  Floor Division
  Order of Operations

<u>Lists</u>   Pgs 36-44
  Creating a List
  About Lists
  List Length
  Accessing Items
  Index Ranges
  Changing an Item

Table of Contents

Changing a Range of Items
Inserting an Item
Adding an Item
Removing an Item
Removing with Index

Tuples   Pgs 46-47
  Creating a Tuple
  Update a Tuple

                                                            Pgs 49-50

Sets
  Intro to Sets
  Adding Values

Dictionaries   Pgs 52-57
  Intro to Dictionaries
  Accessing Values
  Changing Values
  Adding Values
  Removing Values

Table of Contents

<u>If-Else Loops</u> Pgs 59-62
   Intro to If-Else Loops
   Other conditions
   Elif
   And
   Or

<u>While Loops</u> Pg 64
   Intro to While Loops

<u>For Loop</u> Pgs 66-67
   Intro to For Loops
   The range function

<u>Functions</u> Pg 69
   Intro to functions
   Calling a function

Table of Contents

OOP   Pgs 71-73

    What is OOP?
    Introducing Classes
    Intro to Objects
    The init function

Inheritance   Pgs 75-77

    Intro to Inheritance
    Parent Class
    Child Class

Input   Pg 81

    Collecting User Input

How To Use This Book

This book is suitable for beginners of all ages trying to learn to code in Python. It guides you through the basics step by step. As you progress through the book, there are also several advanced functionalities discussed (all with step by step tutorials of course). The table of contents includes a breakdown of the topics so if you are a more advanced learner, you can skip to the pages of interest to you! I would highly encourage you to follow the instructions and type the code on your own, in order to get the most out of this book.

Also, I cannot emphasize enough the importance of saving your code regularly! Remember Ctrl+S (or command if you are a Mac user).

I hope you enjoy this coding journey!

Python Programming: The Ultimate Guide

By: Alisha Aggarwal

"Coding is today's language of creativity" - Maria Klawe

Intro to Python

<u>What is Python?</u>

Python is a programming language that has various applications. It can help solve mathematical problems, categorize information, and even build games. There's so much to discover with Python. So what are you waiting for? Let's learn Python!

Notes

Starting to Code

Where do I Start Coding?

You can start by downloading IDLE.

IDLE (Python 3.9 64-bit)
App

Open ->File->New File->Ctrl+S to Save

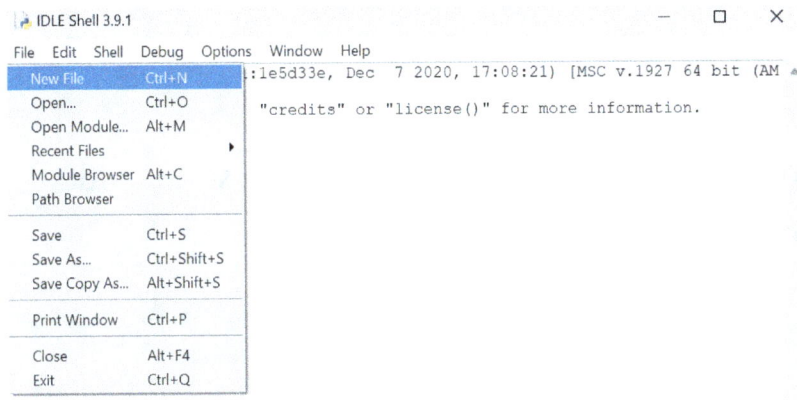

Starting to Code

How do I run my code?

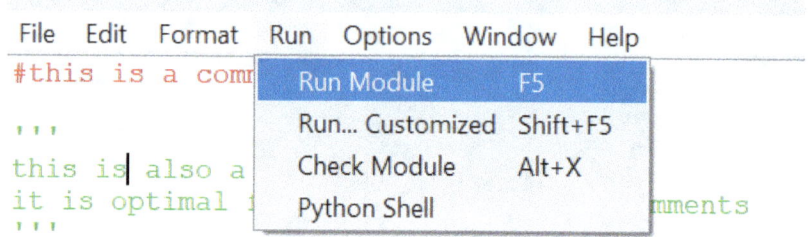

Run -> Run Module

Of course, you can also use the keyboard shortcut F5

Now you're ready to start learning some code that you can run!

Starting to Code

<u>Basic Python Things to be Familiar With</u>

In Python, formatting and indentation are extremely important! Your code can have major problems if your indentation does not match the desired indentation. You do not have to use a tab to indent, however, it is strongly recommended. When indenting, you must have at least one space. Make sure to keep track of you number of spaces because you need to keep it consistent throughout your code.

Another thing to note is the significance of having opening and closing brackets, along with having to start and close quotation marks

Starting to Code

Writing Comments

```
#this is a comment

'''
this is also a commment
it is optimal for having multi line comments
'''
```

Writing comments can come in handy as they can serve as notes or quick reminders about what each section of the code does. Comments are hidden when the program is run. The general structure of a comment is above. Make sure to follow this so you don't get an error when running your code.

Creating a Variable

Python is considered one of the simplest programming languages because of the little syntax (or code) it requires to get the desired output.

Seeing the code for creating a variable on the next page.

Starting to Code

Notice how you don't need to specify the variable type (like an integer), contrary to other syntax-heavy programming languages like Java.

```
x=5
```

It's as simple as that! The variable (defined as 'x') has been assigned the value of the number 5. This won't give you anything when you run the code because the value 5 has been stored for x not been asked to output.

What about storing text? See the code below

```
name="Alisha Aggarwal"
```

But how does the program know that x is given the number value 5 and not text with the number 5 in it? For that, you will need to learn about different data types and casting. You will be exploring these over the next few pages.

Notes

Data Types

String Data Type

A 'String' is used to refer to text. Putting quotation marks around something makes it a string. So if I were to rewrite the code to this, what do you think would happen?

$$x = '5'$$

The variable 'x' would have the string (text) including the number 5 in it. So basically, the program would not recognize x's value to be a number and would give errors if you attempted mathematical calculations with it.

Integer Data Type

An integer is used to refer to any non-decimal number.

$$x = 5$$

This code would be an example of assigning an integer value to something. Be very careful NOT to put quotes around the numbers when assigning unless you want a String!

Data Types

Float Data Type

A 'Float' is used to refer to decimal numbers. Decimals have numbers floating after the decimal point, hence the name.

This code would be an example of assigning a float value to something.

```
z = 9.5
```

Again, be very careful NOT to put quotes around the decimal when assigning unless you want a String! This is very similar to defining integers. Pretty simple right?

Data Types

Boolean Data Type

A 'Boolean' is used to refer to a condition being true or false.

Here is an example of a Boolean statement:

```
loveCoding = True
```

In the code above, the variable called 'loveCoding' has been assigned True. Now, you need to be extremely careful here because if you put quotes around True, then it becomes a String and is no longer recognized as a Boolean.

When naming your variable, make sure it reflects the condition accurately. Also, ensure that you have capitalized either True or False.

Data Types

Print Statements

A 'Print Statement' is used to refer to the display of information when the program is run.

Here is an example of a print statement:

```
print("Python rocks!")
```

The output of the code above can be seen below:

```
Python rocks!
```

In the code above, a String is being returned However, you can also print a value of a variable directly.

See the example below:

```
loveCoding = True

print(loveCoding);
```

Data Types

When your run this code, the output is 'True'

```
True
```

If you chose not to put quotations around loveCoding, then the program would not recognize it as a variable and would not output True.

You can also do the same for other data types such as integers and floats. See the example below:

```
y =-4
z = 9.5
print(y);
print(z);
```

→
```
-4
9.5
```

Notes

More About Variables

Changing Variable Types

You may recall that you do not need to state the variable type when defining one. Did you know that you can also change the variable type after it has been defined? How would you code this? See the example below.

```
x=3

x="Alisha Aggarwal"
```

Here, the variable 'x' has changed from type Integer to type String.

Casting

Although you don't need to specify the variable data type, you certainly can. How can you do this? With casting. See the example code on the next page.

More About Variables

```python
x=str(4)# equals to String type 4
x=float(4) #equals to float type equalling 4.0
x=int(4) #equals to integer type equalling 4
```

Obtaining a Variable's Type

How can you figure out what a variable's type is? See the example below.

```python
x="Alisha Aggarwal"
y = 5
print(type(x))
print(type(y))
```

↓

```
<class 'str'>
<class 'int'>
```

See how when I run the program, I can see the type String (str) and Integer (int).

More About Variables

Naming Variables

If you're coding in Python, chances are that you will be using lots of variables. So here is some advice about variables.

Remember that variable names ARE case-sensitive. So 'var' is NOT the same as 'Var'. Be extremely careful about naming variables. I suggest keeping a consistent method for naming. Generally, coders use something called Camel Case when naming variables. Here's an example with Camel Case.

```
'''If I wanted a variable with the name python code I would write it as:
pythonCode
See what happened here? Everything is lowercase except for the first letter
of the 2nd word AND there are no underscores.
'''

'''
If you are naming a variable that is intended to not change its value then you
would uppercase its name
For example:
RED
'''
```

Try to make the variable name short and meaningful.

More About Variables

Variable Shortcut

What if you wanted to define more than one variable but you didn't want to write a line of code for each one? Is there a quicker way? Yes, there is and you're about to learn about it!

See the example below:

```
x, y, z = "Alisha Aggarwal", 4, "Python"
print(x)
print(y)
print(z)
```

```
Alisha Aggarwal
4
Python
```

More About Variables

Print Shortcut

What if you wanted to print more than one variable but didn't want to occupy too many lines? Is there a quicker way? Yes, there is and you're about to learn about it!

See the example below:

```
x, y, z = "Alisha Aggarwal", 4, "Python"
print(x,y,z)
```

```
Alisha Aggarwal 4 Python
```

Notes

Operators

What is an Operator?

An operator is something that can perform operations on values and variables.

Arithmetic Operators

Arithmetic operators are those used to perform mathematical calculations.

```
'''
These operations will be pretty familiar to you:
add --> +
subtract --> -
divide --> /
mutiply --> *

But wait, there's more!
'''
```

Modulus

Modulus allows you to get the remainder of a division. See the example on the next page to see it in action!

Operators

```
print(10%4)
```

↓

2

This prints the remainder of 10 divided by 4, which equals 2.

<u>Exponents</u>

```
print(2**6)
```

↓

64

This print statement is equivalent to 2 to the power of 6, which gives a result of 64.

Operators

Floor Division

Floor division is essentially division but it truncates the result so only the whole number value is shown. Note: this chops everything after the decimal point - it DOES NOT round so this type of answer may not be the most accurate in some cases.

So how do you do floor division? See the example below.

```
print(15 // 4)
```

↓

3

Operators

Order of Operations

When doing mathematical calculations, it is essential to consider the order of operations so you can obtain your intended output. You may have learned the acronym PEMDAS in school. Let's adapt this acronym to be PEMMDAS.

P: Parenthesis
E: Exponents
MM: Multiplication and Modulus
D: Division
A: Addition
S: Subtraction

Remember that multiplication, modulus, and division's order can depend on which one comes first. The same applies to addition and subtraction.

Notes

Lists

Creating a List

Lists can collect multiple collections of data in one variable.

See the example of creating a list below.

```
groceries = ["apple", "bread","milk", "eggs"]
print(groceries)
```

↓

`['apple', 'bread', 'milk', 'eggs']`

About Lists

The items in lists are ordered. The first item has an index of 0, the second has an index of 1, and so on. The last item has an index of -1.

Lists

List Length

You can use the len function to figure out how many items are in a list. Note: this won't start counting at 0.

See the example below:

```
groceries = ["apple", "bread","milk", "eggs"]
print(len(groceries))
```

↓

Note that lists can also contain a combination of data types.

Lists

Accessing Items

Remember list indexes that you recently learned about? You can use these indexes to obtain specific values from lists.

See the example below:

```
groceries = ["apple", "bread","milk", "eggs"]
print(groceries[2])
```

```
milk
```

Index Ranges

What if you wanted to print a range of numbers from a list?

See the example on the next page.

Lists

```
groceries = ["apple", "bread","milk", "eggs"]
print(groceries[1:3])
```

`['bread', 'milk']`

Note that in the range 1:3, the first index is included and the 3rd index is NOT included. Everything in between IS included, of course.

You can also print a range till the end by including a range like '2: ' (leaving the number after the colon blank).

Lists

Changing an Item

How can you change an item in an existing list?

See the example below.

```
groceries = ["apple", "bread","milk", "eggs"]
groceries[1] = "ice cream"
print(groceries)
```

↓

```
['apple', 'ice cream', 'milk', 'eggs']
```

Changing a Range of Items

How can you change an entire range of items in an existing list?

See the example on the next page.

Lists

```
groceries = ["apple", "bread","milk", "eggs"]
groceries[1:3] = ["ice cream", "huummus"]
print(groceries)
```

```
['apple', 'ice cream', 'huummus', 'eggs']
```

Inserting an Item

First of all, it's very important to make the distinction between inserting values and adding values in a list.

When you add values to a list, they are automatically added to the end of a list. However, when you insert values, you can place them in between the list as per your specification.

How do you insert values in a list?

See the example on the next page.

Lists

```
groceries = ["apple", "bread","milk", "eggs"]
groceries.insert(2, "ice cream")
print(groceries)
```

```
['apple', 'bread', 'ice cream', 'milk', 'eggs']
```

Adding an Item

How do you add values to a list?

See the example below.

```
groceries = ["apple", "bread","milk", "eggs"]
groceries.append("ice cream")
print(groceries)
```

```
['apple', 'bread', 'milk', 'eggs', 'ice cream']
```

Lists

Removing an Item

How do you remove values from a list? Using a remove method!

See the example below.

```python
groceries = ["apple", "bread","milk", "eggs"]
groceries.remove("bread")
print(groceries)
```

↓

```
['apple', 'milk', 'eggs']
```

Removing with Index

What if you wanted to remove an item based on its index value?

See the example on the next page!

Lists

```python
groceries = ["apple", "bread","milk", "eggs"]
groceries.pop(1)
print(groceries)
```

↓

```
['apple', 'milk', 'eggs']
```

Note that you can also choose not to specify any index, in which case the last item in the list gets removed.

Notes

Tuples

Creating a Tuple

So what's a tuple? A tuple is a list but the important difference is that a tuple CANNOT be changed.

How do you create a tuple?

See the example below:

```python
groceries = ("apple", "bread","milk", "eggs")
print(groceries)
```

↓

```
('apple', 'bread', 'milk', 'eggs')
```

You can also use a len function with a tuple, just like lists. Tuples can also include items from different data types. You can also retrieve a tuple item using indexing.

Tuples

Update a Tuple

So what if you wanted to add something to a tuple? Wait a minute, didn't you say that tuples cannot be changed (they are immutable)? Yes, that's true tuples CANNOT directly be changed. But tuples CAN be converted to lists to make changes to them.

How do we convert a tuple to a list? So we can make changes.

See the example below:

```
groceries = ("apple", "bread","milk", "eggs")

groceriesList = list(groceries)
groceriesList[1]="mangoes"
groceries = tuple(groceriesList)

print(groceries)
```

↓

```
('apple', 'mangoes', 'milk', 'eggs')
```

Notes

Sets

Intro to Sets

What is a set? A set is a list BUT it is NOT ordered (which means indexing rules and functions do not apply), you CANNOT have any duplicate items, and you CANNOT insert values.

How do you create a set?

See the example below:

```
groceries = {"apple", "bread","milk", "eggs"}
print(groceries)
```

↓

```
{'apple', 'bread', 'eggs', 'milk'}
```

Note that the values 1 and True are considered duplicates for sets.

The len function still applies and items can still be of a combination of data types.

Sets

Adding Values

Adding values is a bit different with sets than with lists. You don't use the append function. Instead, you use an add function.

How do you add values in a set?

See it in action with the example below:

```
groceries = {"apple", "bread","milk", "eggs"}
groceries.add("maple syrup")

print(groceries)
```

{'milk', 'apple', 'maple syrup', 'bread', 'eggs'}

You can still use the remove method to remove values, just like lists.

Notes

Dictionaries

Intro to Dictionaries

A dictionary is another way of storing collections of data. Depending on your Python version, your dictionary can follow the index rules and functions (ordered) or be unordered. So, if your Python program is 3.6 or earlier, then your dictionaries will be unordered. Else, your Python program will be ordered.

How do you create a dictionary?

See the example below:

```
dict = {
   "fruit": "Mango",
   "shape": "Oval",
   "color": "Yellow",
   "number": 5
}

print(dict)
```

↓

{'fruit': 'Mango', 'shape': 'Oval', 'color': 'Yellow', 'number': 5}

Dictionaries

Duplicate entries are NOT allowed in dictionaries. Dictionaries ARE, however, changeable (mutable). In the case that your dictionary has duplicate values, the most recent instance (or version) of that value will override existing values.

You CAN still use the len function, just like with lists. As you can see in the example on the previous page, dictionaries accept values from different data types.

Now you've learned about all the collection methods in Python. Be sure to carefully consider which one is suitable for your coding occasion.

Dictionaries

Accessing Values

How can you access values in dictionaries?

See the example below:

```python
dict = {
   "fruit": "Mango",
   "shape": "Oval",
   "color": "Yellow",
   "number": 5
}

x = dict["shape"]

print(x)
```

↓

```
Oval
```

Dictionaries

<u>Changing Values</u>

Think of changing values as overriding the existing values.

How can you change values in dictionaries?

See the example below:

```
dict = {
    "fruit": "Mango",
    "shape": "Oval",
    "color": "Yellow",
    "number": 5
}

dict["number"] = 25

print(dict)
```

↓

{'fruit': 'Mango', 'shape': 'Oval', 'color': 'Yellow', 'number': 25}

Dictionaries

Adding Values

Adding values is a bit different in dictionaries than anything that you've seen so far.

How can you add values in dictionaries?

See the example below:

```python
dict = {
    "fruit": "Mango",
    "shape": "Oval",
    "color": "Yellow",
    "number": 5
}

dict["size"] = "small"

print(dict)
```

↓

{'fruit': 'Mango', 'shape': 'Oval', 'color': 'Yellow', 'number': 5, 'size': 'small'}

Dictionaries

<u>Removing Values</u>

Remember the pop method? Well, you'll be using it here too!

How can you add values in dictionaries?

See the example below:

```
dict = {
  "fruit": "Mango",
  "shape": "Oval",
  "color": "Yellow",
  "number": 5
}

dict.pop("color")

print(dict)
```

↓

{'fruit': 'Mango', 'shape': 'Oval', 'number': 5}

Notes

If-Else Loops

Intro to If-Else Loops

If-else loops use conditions to check if something is true or false, and then they act accordingly.

How can you create an if-else loop?

See the example below:
```
a = 238
b = 42
if a >= b:
    print("a is greater than or equal to b")
else:
    print("b is greater than a")
```

a is greater than or equal to b

Note the specific indentation in Python.

If-Else Loops

Other conditions

Here are examples of several other conditions that you can use in if-else loops:

- a==b
    - checks if a equals b
- a!=b
    - checks if a is NOT equal to b
- a<b
    - checks if a is less than b
- a>b
    - checks if a is greater than b
- a<=b
    - checks if a is less than or equal to b

If-Else Loops

Elif

Now that you know the basic structure of an if-else loop, let's introduce elif. First of all, what is elif? Elif is short for else if.

If the if condition is not met, then the program can proceed to elif statement or statements, before finally ending at else.

How can you code this? See the example below.

```python
a = 238
b = 42
if a > b:
    print("a is greater than b")
elif a==b:
    print("a is equal to b")
else:
    print("b is greater than a")
```

If-Else Loops

And

You can also use the 'and' keyword to combine conditions and check them at the same time in if-else loops.

How can you code this? See the example below.

```
a = 238
b = 42
c=78
if a > b and c<a:
    print("a is greater than b AND c is less than a")
```

Or

Similarly, there is also an or keyword that checks if a condition or if another condition is true in an if-else loop. See the example above and try incorporating or on your own!

Notes

While Loops

Intro to While Loops

While loops iterate (repeat) code until a certain condition is met.

How can you code this? See the example below.

```
i = 4
while i < 20: #condition to keep going until
    print(i)
    i += 2 #update the value of i each time the loop runs
```

You also add an else statement after a while loop!

That was a nice, short, and easy lesson, huh?

Notes

For Loop

Intro to For Loops

A for loop is used for repeating (iterating) a set of code over and over again.

How can you code this? See the example below.

```
for x in "Alisha Aggarwal":
    print(x)
```

↓

```
A
l
i
s
h
a

A
g
g
a
r
w
a
l
```

For Loop

The range function

The range function can allow you to specify the number of times you want the code to run.

How can you code this? See the example below.

```
i = 0
for i in range(11):#11 times the code will run
    print(i)
    i+=1 #updates i's value each time the loop runs (this adds by 1 each time)
```

0
1
2
3
4
5
6
7
8
9
10

Notes

Functions

Intro to Functions

A function allows you to define code to call to run later on.

How can you code this? See the example below.

```python
def function():
    print("My first function!")
```

Calling a Function

You may have noticed that the above code doesn't do anything, even though there is a print statement included. That's because you haven't called the function yet!

See the code below to call a function!

```python
def function():
    print("My first function!")

function()
```

Notes

OOP

What is OOP?

OOP stands for Object Oriented Programming. You will learn how to do object-oriented programming in Python. OOP means that there are objects and classes. This helps with decreasing the number of lines of code and makes you a more efficient programmer. Starting from this point, these tutorials will be more advanced. Don't worry, all this will start making more sense later on.

Introducing Classes

A class allows for the creation of objects. To create a class, you will need to use the class keyword. Make sure that class is lowercase for your code to work!

How can you create a class? See the example code on the next page.

OOP

```
class MyClass:
    a = "Alisha Aggarwal"
```

Intro to Objects

An object is like a version of a class that can use information from the class to carry out certain actions.

How can you code an object? See the example below.

```
class MyClass:
    a = "Alisha Aggarwal"

object1 = MyClass()
print(object1.a)
```

Alisha Aggarwal

OOP

The init function

You were just learning the basics of objects and classes. Now it's time to start learning how to apply these for code efficiency! The init function initializes the properties of a class.

How can you code an init function? See the example below.

```python
class Person:
   def __init__(self, name, age):
      self.name = name
      self.age = age
      self.height = height

alisha = Person()
print(alisha.age)
```

Notes

Inheritance

<u>Intro to Inheritance</u>

So what is inheritance? No, I am not talking about getting money after someone passed away. Also no, I am not talking about you getting certain genes from your parents. In Python, inheritance is different. However, the principle is just like the alternate definitions I mentioned above.

In inheritance, there are parent classes and child classes. You will be learning more about these soon!

You may be thinking why inheritance? Like, I understand why OOP is so helpful but what's the purpose of inheritance? Inheritance is also another way of increasing efficiency. Different classes can inherit code segments from other classes saving you from writing lots of code!

Inheritance

Parent Class

A parent class is also known as a base class. This is the class which code is inherited from.

How can you code a parent class? Well, any class can take the form of a parent class. Guess what! You've already learned the code for it!

Child Class

A child class is also known as a derived class. This is a class that inherits code from a parent class. A child class is a subclass of a parent class.

How can you code a child class/? Beware, the syntax for this one is different that that of a parent class! See the example code on the next page.

Inheritance

```
class Author(Person):
    pass
```

The author class is a child class that will inherit code from the parent class (which is the person class in this case). Notice how the keyword class is lowercase but the name of the class always has the first letter capitalized.

Note that using the keyword pass is not necessary to create a child class - it has simply been done in this example. The purpose of the keyword pass is to indicate that no other methods are being added.

be careful! If you add an init function to the child class, then it will no longer inherit it from the parent class because the new init function will override the inherited code.

Notes

Input

Collecting User Input

In order to really make a program shine, it needs to have interaction with the user. Well, you can't do that without the input function!

How do you code the input function? See the example code below:

```
name = input("Tell me your name: ")
print("Nice to meet you " + name)
```

```
Tell me your name: Alisha
Nice to meet you Alisha
```

Inputs are also great for chatbots!

Notes

About the Author

Alisha Aggarwal has experience in 7 programming languages: HTML, CSS, JavaScript, Python, Java, Arduino, and SQL. She has achieved perfect scores in several coding competitions and has also come 1st place.

She first started with Scratch when she was 9 and then coded in her first text-based language, HTML at age 11. She is passionate about coding and strives to inspire others to learn to code. She aims to encourage others to develop their programming skills and wishes for a more equal gender distribution in technology-related fields.

Be sure to check out all her other publications - you can learn about them over the next few pages!

Message From the Author

Being able to code is one of the greatest gifts in the world. It is amazing how much one can accomplish through this. Coding is a skill that can be developed through practice. Never stop dreaming and work hard to turn your dreams into reality. Don't give up and believe in yourself. Trust the process. You can achieve anything you set your mind to no matter how hard it seems!

Check Out the Author's Other Work

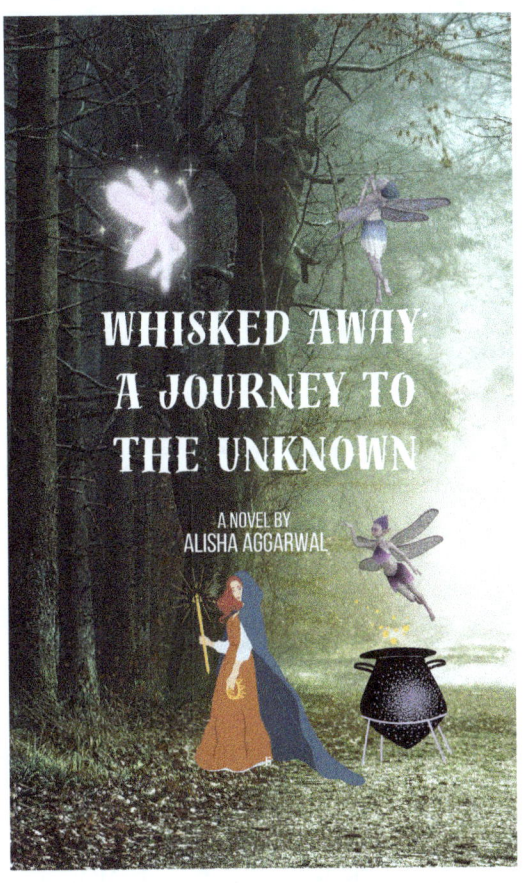

Whisked Away: A Journey to the Unknown dives into the adventure of 15-year-old Aubrey, as she finds herself in a mysterious place with no sign of home. This book includes eye-catching graphics that complement the words and is designed for elementary and middle schoolers interested in fantasy.

ONLY $10 on Amazon.com

Check Out the Author's Other Work

This book is intended for anyone interested in lettering, whether they be a beginner or have some experience. This book serves as a guide from proper lettering materials to basic alphabet practice to techniques to various projects and styles. There is something for everyone and if you feel you don't associate with a particular style, feel free to come up with your own!

Hardcover AND Paperback Versions Available on Amazon.com

Check Out the Author's Other Work

HTML & CSS: The Ultimate Guide

By: Alisha Aggarwal

This book is suitable for beginners of all ages trying to learn to code in HTML, CSS, and aiming to learn about website development. It guides you through the basics step by step. As you progress through the book, there are also several advanced functionalities discussed (all with step by step tutorials of course). The table of contents includes a breakdown of the topics so if you are a more advanced learner, you can skip to the pages of interest to you!

Available on Amazon.com: ONLY $9.42

www.ingramcontent.com/pod-product-compliance
Lightning Source LLC
Chambersburg PA
CBHW051540240526
45465CB00028B/1709